Mission: Space Science

Unlocking the Secrets of the Solar System

Megan Kopp

CRABTREE
PUBLISHING COMPANY
WWW.CRABTREEBOOKS.COM

Mission: Space Science

Author: Megan Kopp

Editors: Sarah Eason, Tim Cooke, Ellen Rodger

Editorial director: Kathy Middleton

Design: Paul Myerscough and Lynne Lennon

Cover design: Paul Myerscough

Photo research: Rachel Blount

Proofreader and indexer: Nancy Dickmann, Wendy Scavuzzo

Production coordinator and prepress technician: Ken Wright

Print coordinator: Katherine Berti

Consultant: David Hawksett

Produced for Crabtree Publishing by Calcium Creative

Photo Credits:
t=Top, tr=Top Right, tl=Top Left

Inside: NASA: pp. 7, 11, 12, 14, 18, 20, 21, 24, 26, 29, 32, 33, 34, 35, 39, 40, 44; ESA / ATG medialab: p. 36; ESA / Herschel / PACS / MESS Key Programme Supernova Remnant Team; NASA, ESA and Allison Loll / Jeff Hester (Arizona State University): p. 28; ESA / NASA / JPL / University of Arizona: p. 41; NASA / Bill Ingalls: p. 16; JHUAPL / SwRI: pp. 1, 22, 27; NASA / Johns Hopkins University Applied Physics Laboratory / Carnegie Institution of Washington: p. 25; NASA / JPL: p. 45; NASA / JPL-Caltech / GSFC / JAXA: p. 8; NASA / JPL-Caltech / T. Pyle (SSC): p. 31; NASA / JPL-Caltech / SwRI / MSSS / Gerald Eichstad / Sean Doran: p. 23; NASA / JPL / University of Arizona / Los Alamos National Laboratories: p. 19; NASA / JPL-Caltech / UCLA / MPS / DLR / IDA: p. 37; Kim Shiflett: p. 30; Shutterstock: Luca Flor: p. 10; Elgin Green: p 13; Alex Mit: p. 5; Jurik Peter: p. 43; Solarseven: p. 9; SSSCCC: p. 15; Marilyn Volan: p. 4; Wikimedia Commons: Go Miyazaki: p. 6; NASA: p. 42; NASA / Johns Hopkins APL / Steve Gribben: p. 17; NASA / Johns Hopkins University Applied Physics Laboratory / Southwest Research Institute / Steve Gribben: p. 38.

Cover: Shutterstock: Vadim Sadovski.

Library and Archives Canada Cataloguing in Publication

Kopp, Megan, author
Unlocking the secrets of the solar system / Megan Kopp.

(Mission: space science)
Includes index.
Issued in print and electronic formats.
ISBN 978-0-7787-5396-4 (hardcover).--
ISBN 978-0-7787-5407-7 (softcover).--
ISBN 978-1-4271-2211-7 (HTML)

1. Solar system--Juvenile literature.
2. Outer space--Juvenile literature. I. Title.

QB501.3.K67 2019 j523.2 C2018-906112-X
C2018-906113-8

Library of Congress Cataloging-in-Publication Data

Names: Kopp, Megan, author.
Title: Unlocking the secrets of the solar system / Megan Kopp.
Other titles: Solar system
Description: New York, New York : Crabtree Publishing Company, [2019] |
Series: Mission: space science | Includes index.
Identifiers: LCCN 2018050352 (print) |
LCCN 2018057701 (ebook) |
ISBN 9781427122117 (Electronic) |
ISBN 9780778753964 (hardcover) |
ISBN 9780778754077 (pbk.)
Subjects: LCSH: Solar system--Juvenile literature |
Planets--Juvenile literature.
Classification: LCC QB501.3 (ebook) |
LCC QB501.3 .K67 2019 (print) | DDC 523.2--dc23
LC record available at https://lccn.loc.gov/2018050352

Crabtree Publishing Company
www.crabtreebooks.com 1-800-387-7650

Printed in the U.S.A./032019/CG20190118

Published in Canada
Crabtree Publishing
616 Welland Ave.
St. Catharines, Ontario
L2M 5V6

Published in the United States
Crabtree Publishing
PMB 59051
350 Fifth Avenue, 59th Floor
New York, New York 10118

Published in the United Kingdom
Crabtree Publishing
Maritime House
Basin Road North, Hove
BN41 1WR

Published in Australia
Crabtree Publishing
Unit 3 – 5
Currumbin Court
Capalaba QLD 4157

Contents

CHAPTER 1

What Is the Solar System?

A **solar system** is a star and the objects that travel around it, including **planets**, **asteroids**, and **comets**. Our Solar System centers on the Sun. The Sun's **gravity**, a force that attracts objects, holds Earth and other planets and objects in **orbit** around it. Some planets are orbited by **moons**. Mercury is the closest planet to the Sun. One of the most distant objects is Sedna. It is not classified as a planet. It is one of the many objects in the outer reaches of our Solar System.

A **galaxy** is a clump of billions of solar systems. Our Solar System is in the Milky Way galaxy. This is a spiral-shaped galaxy that contains several hundred billion stars, including our Sun. The Milky Way is about 100,000 **light-years** across. A light-year is the distance light travels in a year, which is around 5.9 trillion miles (9.5 trillion km). On a dark night, you can sometimes see the Milky Way as a thick band of stars in the sky. Our Solar System is in one of the galaxy's four spiral arms.

This artwork shows the order of the planets in our Solar System in relation to the Sun.

In a galaxy such as the Milky Way, stars and their solar systems are bunched in long arms that form a flat spiral shape.

Many stars have planets circling around them. There could be billions of other planets in the Milky Way alone. Some solar systems possess more than one star. **Binary star systems** have two stars. **Multi-star systems** have three or more stars in one solar system.

Chasing Space

In the United States, the National Aeronautics and Space Administration (NASA) improves our understanding of the Solar System by exploring the planets, their moons, and small bodies such as comets. Its research seeks to learn about the **origin**, or beginning, and history of our Solar System. NASA scientists are also looking out for the possibility that life exists elsewhere in space. The 2018 Global Exploration Roadmap is a document that shows the plan of 14 space agencies that have come together with a common goal to expand human presence in our Solar System. The plan starts with missions to the International Space Station (ISS), which orbits Earth, then advances to the Moon, and then to Mars. Cooperation between the agencies will be the key to success.

Hayabusa2's mission has been to study Ryugu and to also carry four separate landers to investigate the comet's surface.

Why Explore?

Our Solar System is made up of the Sun, eight planets and their moons, at least five **dwarf planets**, millions of asteroids, and probably billions of comets. Despite knowing all this about our Solar System, however, there are still many unanswered questions. There is a lot to discover. Human and **robotic** exploration will help find answers.

Learning More

The Japanese Hayabusa2 spacecraft arrived at the asteroid Ryugu on June 27, 2018. A few months later, it sent a lander to collect samples from the asteroid. After Hayabusa2 left the asteroid, it began to travel back to Earth. When it arrives, scientists will study the samples the spacecraft collected. These samples may help them understand how asteroids formed in the early years of our Solar System. Research such as this expands our understanding of our Solar System.

Focus of Innovation

Space exploration also helps drive new ideas on Earth. Some of the technology developed to build the spacecraft and have it land on an asteroid will filter down to have an impact on different aspects of everyday life.

Its influence could include anything from new materials for the transportation industry to communications systems and advances in computer technology.

New Partnerships

The challenges of exploring space are driving new partnerships between governments, industries, universities, and research centers around the world. Hayabusa2's lander, MASCOT, is operated by the German Aerospace Center (DLR) and the French Space Agency (FSA). The agencies consulted 100 international and national partners before choosing a final landing site on Ryugu.

MISSION:

Space Science

NASA's OSIRIS-REx was launched in September 2016 to land on an asteroid named Bennu just over two years later. Bennu is a small asteroid, measuring 1,600 feet (488 m) in diameter. It was selected as a target from more than 500,000 known asteroids because it is close to Earth. Its ancient rocks may hold clues to the origin of life. Its surface of loose soil, dust, and broken rock should be easy for a lander to collect. OSIRIS-REx returned its first images of Bennu in August 2018, when it was still 1.4 million miles (2.2 million km) away.

This artwork imagines asteroids surrounding a young planet when our Solar System was new.

CHAPTER 2

The Sun

Like about 10 percent of the other stars in the Milky Way galaxy, our Sun is a **yellow dwarf** star. A yellow dwarf is a medium-sized star. The Sun is a bright, hot ball made up of **hydrogen** and **helium**. Hydrogen undergoes a nuclear reaction to form helium, generating heat at the same time. The Sun is 864,000 miles (1.4 milion km) in diameter. That is more than 100 times as wide as Earth. Around 1.3 million Earths would fit inside the Sun. Temperatures on the Sun range from 10,000 °Fahrenheit (5,540 °C) on the surface to around 27 million °Fahrenheit (15 million °C) at the center.

Superstrong Sun

The Sun holds our Solar System together. Its gravity keeps everything in orbit, from large planets such as Jupiter to tiny pieces of space dust. Earth is only the third planet from the Sun, and it is 93 million miles (150 million km) away. Distances in our Solar System are usually measured in **astronomical units (AU)**. One AU is the distance from Earth to the Sun. Neptune is about 30 AU from the Sun. Sedna is another orbiting object discovered in 2003. Its distance from the Sun varies between 76 AU and 940 AU. The Sun and the rest of our Solar System formed

In this view of the Sun's surface, the bright spots are giant storms on the Sun that are bigger than Earth.

The Sun releases more energy in 1.5 millionths of a second than everyone on Earth uses in a year.

from a giant, spinning cloud of gas and dust about 4.5 billion years ago. There was so much gravity that the cloud collapsed in on itself, spinning faster and faster and flattening out. Most of the material was pulled toward the center. It formed our Sun, and the other material formed the planets, moons, and other objects. The Sun makes up 99.8 percent of the **mass** of our entire Solar System.

Copycats

Hydrogen makes up most of the Sun's mass. It is under so much pressure that hydrogen **atoms** hit each other with such force that they blend together to form a different **element** called helium. This process is called **nuclear fusion**, and it releases vast amounts of energy. Scientists are trying to scale down this process so they can use it in a new wave of nuclear fusion **reactors** to produce electricity here on Earth.

The Sun and Earth

Earth has an imaginary line called an **axis** running right through it, from south to north. Earth spins around this axis, making one complete turn every day. But the axis is not straight up and down—it tilts to one side. As Earth orbits the Sun, the tilt of the axis does not change. At any point during the year, some parts of Earth are tilted toward the Sun, while others are tilted away. Those areas pointing toward the Sun get direct rays and warmer weather. This is what causes the seasons.

The Sun does not heat our planet evenly. In different seasons, different amounts of sunlight hit the surface. Areas near the **equator** get the most energy from sunlight, while areas near the **poles** get the least. These differences create movement in the **atmosphere**, which is the envelope of gas surrounding Earth. Along with Earth's rotation, it drives movements in the ocean known as **currents**. The ocean and the atmosphere affect the **water cycle** and influence our **climate** and weather.

In winter (top left) and fall (bottom right), Earth receives less sunlight than in spring (top right) and summer (bottom left).

Solar storms are periods of rapid change on the surface of the Sun. They cause huge eruptions of energy.

Sun Seasons?

Scientists have discovered that our Sun has seasons of its own. It goes through a regular 11-year cycle of being more active then less active. Scientists have discovered that it also has another cycle that lasts just less than a year. This cycle affects space weather and solar storms. Researchers at the National Center for Atmospheric Research (NCAR) have recently developed a model that shows how the seasonal changes begin. It lets scientists forecast seasonal changes in the Sun up to a year ahead of time. This is helpful because high activity on the surface of the Sun can cause problems on Earth. The information is also another clue in understanding how our Sun works. Understanding our star will help scientists understand other stars in our galaxy and beyond.

YOUR MISSION

Observatories study the Sun from many locations. Those near the equator receive similar amounts of sunshine all year around, while others receive less sunshine in winter than in summer. What different information might astronomers learn from different places?

Eclipsed!

An **eclipse** is an event in which a planet or a moon blocks the Sun's light. A **solar eclipse** happens when the Moon gets in the way of the Sun's light and casts its shadow on Earth. When the Moon completely covers the Sun, it is called a **total eclipse**. This happens around every 18 months, but is only visible in certain parts of the world each time. Partial eclipses, when the Moon blocks part of the Sun, happen at least twice a year. When Earth blocks the sunlight that normally hits the Moon, it is called a **lunar eclipse**. Instead of light hitting the Moon's surface, Earth's shadow falls on it and the Moon seems to go dark. Lunar eclipses only happen during a full moon. They can be seen from Earth.

The Moon blocks out part of the Sun as a solar eclipse begins, plunging parts of Earth into darkness.

Why Study Eclipses?

In 2011, NASA's Lunar Reconnaissance Orbiter gathered data about how quickly the Moon cools when Earth blocks the sunlight. Flatter areas of the surface cooled more quickly than areas with many rocks. The data helped scientists map out flat and rough areas on the Moon. Solar eclipses allow scientists to study the Sun's **corona**. This is the sun's fiery outermost layer. It is usually not visible because the Sun's face is far brighter. During the few minutes of a total solar eclipse, the corona is visible around the rim of the Moon. Studying the corona with special instruments gives scientists a better understanding of how the Sun works.

Eclipse 2017

Researchers around the world studied a solar eclipse on August 21, 2017. One study involved a pair of jets equipped with special **telescopes**.

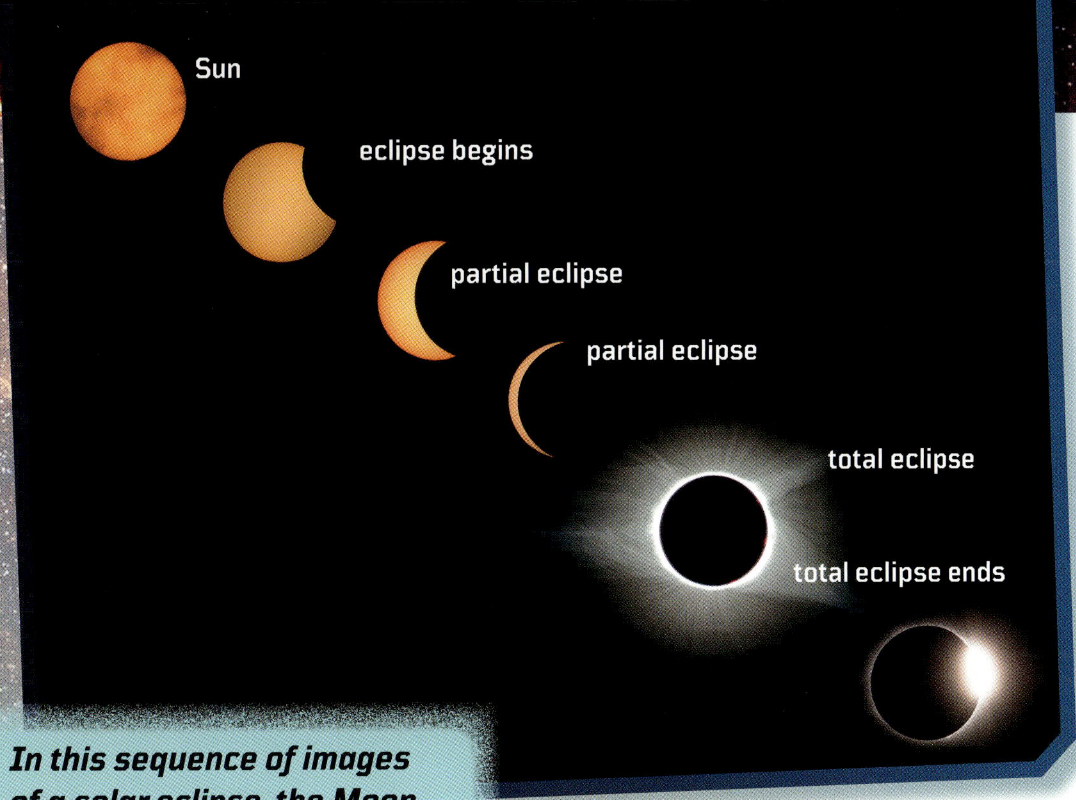

In this sequence of images of a solar eclipse, the Moon slowly blocks the Sun, then moves away again.

The planes followed the shadow of the eclipse and stretched its duration to more than 7.5 minutes. Almost four months after the solar eclipse, scientists began sharing the first results from the data collected. Researchers uncovered new information about why the Sun's atmosphere is so hot. They captured detailed images of the **solar winds**, which are caused by billions of tiny electrically charged particles streaming away from the Sun. Scientists also saw cooler blobs of gas in the hot outer corona.

MISSION:

Space Science

High in Earth's upper atmosphere is an area called the **ionosphere**. Here, the Sun's intense energy creates a layer of **ions**, or electrified particles. These changes can affect communications and **navigation signals**, which help pinpoint locations on Earth. One team studied the effect of the eclipse on radio signals. The range of radio signals expanded. There were fewer **energized particles**, or particles carrying solar energy, to interfere with the signals.

Living with a Star

The Sun rules all aspects of our lives on Earth. Understanding how it was formed, how it works, and how it affects us is an important part of space science. NASA has a program called Living With a Star (LWS). It explores the relationships between the Sun and Earth and the rest of our Solar System. In particular, it highlights the science needed to understand those parts of the Sun and space that directly affect Earth. The first LWS mission began with the launch of the Solar Dynamics Observatory in 2010. The observatory is studying the Sun's **magnetic field**. It is hoped it will answer questions such as what causes the magnetic field and how it stores energy. How is energy released as **radiation**, or energy that travels through space?

In this image from the ISS, the Sun shines down on the top of Earth's clouds.

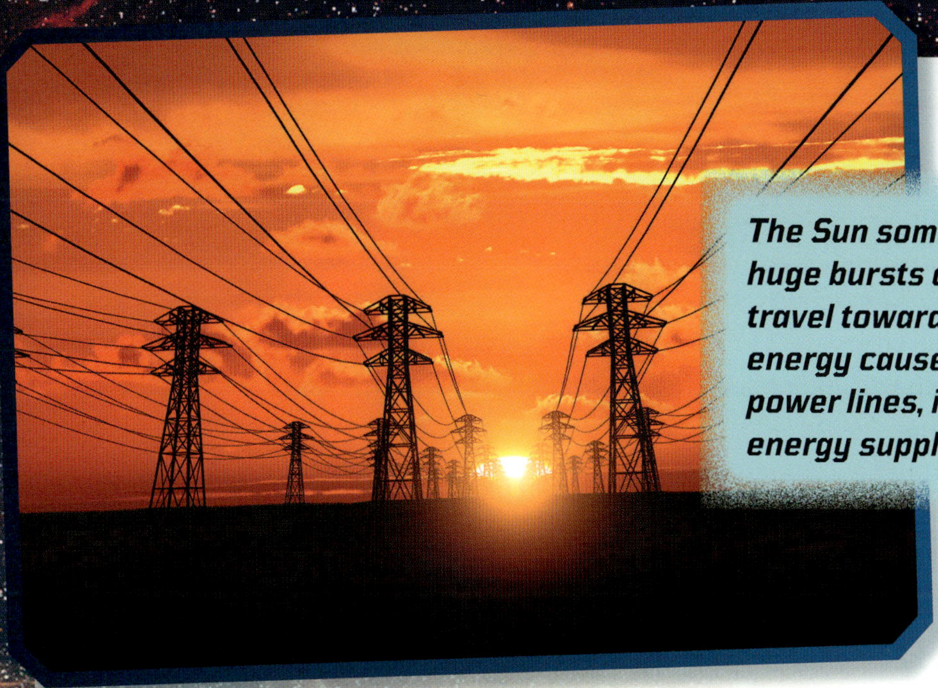

The Sun sometimes releases huge bursts of energy that travel toward Earth. The energy causes surges in power lines, interrupting energy supplies on Earth.

NASA launched twin Radiation Belt Storm **Probes**, or robotic spacecraft, in 2012. They are studying how high-energy particles in space can affect **satellites** and aircraft. The probes are also trying to learn how this energy might affect the health of astronauts on long-distance space missions.

Worldwide Research

The Solar Orbiter (SolO) is a Sun-observing satellite on which NASA is collaborating with the European Space Agency (ESA). It will carry 10 state-of-the-art instruments to observe the stormy surface of the Sun. It will also study the changes that take place in the solar wind that flows out from the Sun at high speeds. The orbiter is scheduled to launch in 2020. It will be the first satellite to offer close-up views of the Sun's polar regions, which are difficult to observe from Earth.

Space Weather

The Sun is constantly sending out a stream of charged particles called the solar wind. These bursts of energy sometimes travel toward Earth. They cause disturbances in space, which in turn affect our upper atmosphere. This energy is responsible for the **auroras**, which are colorful displays of light in the night sky. It can also cause radiation hazards for astronauts on the ISS and other spacecraft. It even causes currents in the ground that **corrode** oil pipelines.

A Solar Probe

A new team member is already up in the skies, checking out our Solar System. NASA and the Johns Hopkins University Applied Physics Lab launched the Parker Solar Probe spacecraft on August 12, 2018. The probe was designed to fly closer to the Sun's surface than any spacecraft before. It will swoop into the Sun's scorching hot atmosphere for a sneak peek of the superhot star that rules our Solar System. Parker is headed for the solar corona. Creating a probe that would survive the hostile conditions near the Sun took a lot of creative thinking.

Taking the Heat

Scientists protect the spacecraft with a heat shield that will not melt as it dips into the Sun's corona. They built a heat shield that can withstand temperatures up to 2,498 °Fahrenheit (1,370 °C). The Sun-facing side is painted white to reflect sunlight. A special black collar between the shield and the probe helps remove excess heat. The probe relies on collecting light energy from **solar panels**. The panels will face sunlight 475 times more intense than on Earth. Water tubes run through the solar panels. They absorb heat from the

The Parker Solar Probe took off from Cape Canaveral in Florida on a Delta IV Heavy rocket.

Near the Sun, the Parker Solar Probe will travel at up to 430,000 miles per hour (692,000 kph).

panels and release it back into space. To make Parker's scientific instruments, engineers experimented with a variety of materials and **alloys**, which are mixes of metals. They tested that the samples would not melt in the world's largest **solar furnace** in France.

Seeing Clearly

Another worry is dust. Parker has twin telescopes. One faces to the front of the probe. One looks behind. Massive dust storms in space hit the telescopes at speeds of up to 105 miles per hour (170 kph). At those speeds, even tiny dust particles can pit the telescope's lens. Just a few pits can spoil the telescope's view, so the team needed to find a type of glass that was tough enough to withstand being hit by dust particles. By 2019, scientists will be receiving a steady stream of data that will help them start to unlock more of the Sun's secrets.

CHAPTER 3

Talking About Planets

What are planets? The answer is not simple. Pluto was once labeled as a planet, for example, but it was reclassified. All planets must orbit the Sun. They must also have enough gravity to keep them nearly round in shape. Pluto meets these conditions, but there are other large objects sharing its orbit. A planet must be large enough to be able to keep any objects of a similar size away from its orbit around the Sun.

Planets grow over millions of years by adding new material. Almost all of this growth occurred billions of years ago in the early Solar System. Smaller masses crashed into each other and joined to form larger bodies, generating heat. Rock melted and became fiery oceans of **magma**, or melted rock. Gases and material were gained and lost. The planet's make-up changed. The order of planets in our Solar System reflects the way our Solar System formed.

This illustration combines images of the planets and the largest four of Jupiter's moons, taken by space probes including Voyager.

When our Solar System was young, only rocky material could stand the heat of the Sun. The **inner planets** (those closer to the Sun)—Mercury, Venus, Earth, and Mars—are rocky. Gravity pulled gases and liquids together to form Jupiter and Saturn. Farther from the Sun, icy substances created the other two **outer planets**, Uranus and Neptune.

In this artwork, the Odyssey probe uses radar to detect ice beneath the surface of Mars.

Baby Planets

In 2018, **astronomers** discovered some of the youngest planets in our galaxy. Using the Atacama Large Millimeter Array (ALMA) in Chile, scientists are studying the gas- and dust-filled areas around young stars, where planets are born. They use a new technique to identify unusual gas-flow patterns. If there are no planets, gas moves around a star in a regular pattern. Gases in a star system normally spin at about 3 miles per second (5 km/s). ALMA can detect changes in gas speed of about 6.5 feet per second (2 m/s). Disturbances in the pattern are signs of planets. The researchers noticed these signs and soon discovered a young star orbited by three newly formed planets.

Life on Mars

Exploration of our Solar System began with uncrewed probes. Humans then set foot on the Moon. The next step is Mars. Finding **resources** there to support human life is critical. In 2018, scientists announced that a spacecraft orbiting Mars had detected a lake of liquid water below the Red Planet's ice sheets. Using ice-penetrating radar, the orbiter flew over the ice sheet from 2012 to 2015. The radar images showed a bright spot that researchers believe to be a lake about 12.5 miles (20 km) wide. Such a lake could prove vital to a future Mars colony. It might also hold **bacteria** and other tiny life forms. Therefore, scientists need to be careful. They need to protect any existing life on Mars.

Life on Mars

Most life on Earth does not exist without support at temperatures below –40 °Fahrenheit (–40 °C). Temperatures below the Martian ice sheet are believed to be about –90 °Fahrenheit (–68 °C). If the lake on Mars has water, it must be extremely salty to remain liquid at such cold temperatures. Could life have **evolved**, or developed, on Mars to live in these conditions?

The spacecraft Odyssey has been in orbit above Mars since 2001. It has made many discoveries about the planet.

The twin rovers Spirit and Opportunity landed on Mars in 2004. Rovers travel over a planet's surface.

To find out for sure, scientists would need to use probes to drill through the ice. However, this risks **contaminating** the lake and could destroy any life that might exist.

Studying Gas

In April 2018, the ESA ExoMars Trace Gas Orbiter started studying **methane**, a colorless gas, in the southern ice sheets. The presence of this gas and water would be more proof that life could exist here. Another recent study suggests that the early Martian surface had only small patches of ice. It was relatively warm and prone to rain.

MISSION:

Space Science

Researchers at the University of Colorado Boulder, discovered **microbes** living in a **toxic**, or poisonous, lake on a volcano here on Earth. Laguna Caliente in Costa Rica's Poás Volcano is 10 million times more **acidic** than tap water. Its water reaches near boiling temperatures. The scientists found a species of bacteria living there. If life can exist in such an extreme environment, they reasoned, it could also exist on Mars.

NASA's New Horizons spacecraft flies past Jupiter and one of its moons.

Jumpin' Jupiter

Orbiting probes have studied the gas giant Jupiter for decades. In 2018, a new study realized that a space traveler may be nestled in Jupiter's orbit. This is the first known asteroid that may have traveled from another star system. Scientists named it 2015 BZ509. The asteroid would not be the only visitor, however. The **interstellar** asteroid 'Oumuamua was spotted in 2017, but it kept on moving and passed right through our Solar System. By contrast, 2015 BZ509 is here to stay. Although it is held captive by Jupiter's gravity, the asteroid moves in the opposite direction from most objects in our Solar System. Researchers have tracked the location of 2015 BZ509 back 4.5 billion years. They believe its odd movement may show it was captured from another solar system.

A Fresh Look

NASA launched the Juno spacecraft in 2011. Five years later, it went into orbit around Jupiter, where it remains.

Juno took this photograph of chaotic patterns in the clouds above Jupiter, caused by storms in the atmosphere.

Roughly every two months, the spacecraft swings close enough to the planet to study its origin, structure, weather, and other scientific features. From the data sent back to Earth, scientists at the Southwest Research Institute in Texas have discovered that the orange and white bands that make up Jupiter's outer atmosphere actually reach thousands of miles deep into the planet's atmosphere.

Researchers have also found masses of **cyclones** circling around Jupiter's poles. A cyclone is a rotating wind system. At the north pole alone, eight separate cyclones rotate around a central cyclone. The outer storms range from 2,500 to 2,900 miles (4,025–4,670 km) across. The south pole has a central cyclone surrounded by five cyclones. These range from 3,500 to 4,300 miles (5,630–6,920 km) in diameter. These storms are unlike anything else in our Solar System. Visible and **infrared** images, which depict an invisible form of light, show the cyclones to have wind speeds up to 220 miles per hour (354 kph). The weather reaches 1,900 miles (3,060 km) down from the outer atmosphere.

New Moons

Mercury and Venus have no moons, and Earth has just one. Jupiter is the moon champion. Astronomers recently discovered another 10 moons orbiting the gas giant. This brings Jupiter's total to a whopping 79 moons. The latest discovery was made in spring 2017, but it was only published in 2018 after it had been confirmed.

Math on Mercury

Planetary scientists rely on a lot of math to complete their work. In 2018, they used new mathematical **formulas**, or calculations, to come up with a new estimate for the thickness of Mercury's crust. Mercury is small, travels fast, and is close to the hot Sun. Visiting it to collect data is a challenge. In 1974 and 1975, the Mariner 10 probe flew past the planet three times, but only one probe has ever orbited the planet. NASA's MErcury Surface, Space ENvironment, GEochemistry, and Ranging mission (MESSENGER) went into orbit around Mercury in 2011. Its mission ended four years later, in 2015.

This image of Mercury has been colored to show different types of rocks and minerals, which are hard substances.

MESSENGER gave researchers a new understanding of how Mercury formed and evolved. It allowed them to map the surface of the entire planet. They estimated Mercury's crust to be about 22 miles (35 km) thick. A scientist from the University of Arizona tried using a different formula in 2018. The new estimate is that Mercury's crust is only 16 miles (26 km) thick. This supports the idea that the crust was formed by volcanic activity. The crust includes different sorts of rocks. Of the rocky planets, Mercury has the largest **core**, or center, for its size. Its core makes up well over half of the planet. Earth's core takes up only 15 percent of the planet.

Another Mission

Scientists looked again at data from Mariner 10's Mercury **flybys** together with MESSENGER's more recent results. Earth-based telescopes also continue to build on our understanding of Mercury. The updated information provides new perspectives. The MESSENGER mission helped pave the way for future missions. ESA and the Japan Aerospace Exploration Agency (JAXA) launched the BepiColombo mission in October 2018. In December 2025, the spacecraft will settle into orbit around Mercury, where it will spend a year. BepiColombo will build on MESSENGER's results. It could also break new ground that will lead to new discoveries.

YOUR MISSION

BepiColombo will be the third probe to visit Mercury. Scientists will compare the data it gathers with data from the two earlier missions. Why do you think going back over old data might be useful? Is it possible for scientists ever to really "know" something about a distant planet, or will new information always change our ideas? Explain your reasons.

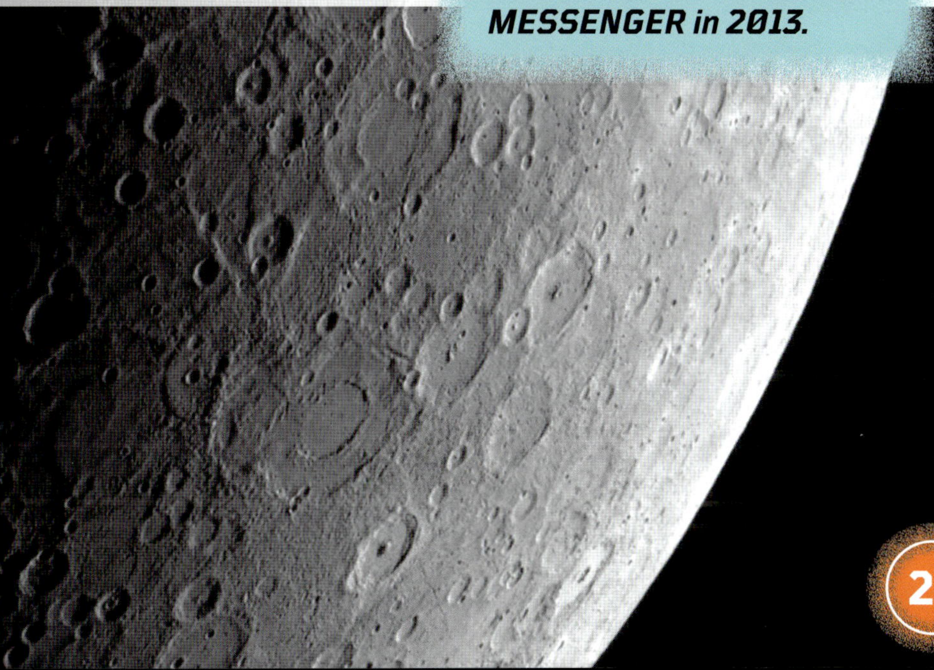

This image of the rocky craters, or round dents, on Mercury was taken by MESSENGER in 2013.

Pluto's Icy Dunes

When Pluto was discovered in 1930, it was identified as the ninth planet in our Solar System. In 2006, it was reclassified as a dwarf planet. That does not mean, however, that scientists are no longer interested in it. The surface of Pluto is extremely cold and dark. It is thought to have a rocky core surrounded by a layer of ice. The temperature on Pluto can be as cold as -375 to -400 °Fahrenheit (-226 to -240 °C). Pluto has mountains, too—made not of rocks but of ice.

In 2018, scientists made an exciting discovery. Using images taken by the New Horizons probe, they found dunes of frozen methane. Like sand dunes on Earth, Pluto's dunes are formed by the wind piling up small grains, though they are grains of methane ice rather than sand. Understanding how these dunes form on Pluto will help scientists understand similar features elsewhere in our Solar System.

Cool Formation

Pluto has a thin and fragile atmosphere that forms when it comes closer to the Sun and disappears as it moves farther away. When Pluto is closest to the Sun, its surface ice changes directly from solid to gas. Pluto becomes much colder during the part of each year when it is traveling far away from the Sun, and the gas then turns solid. This type of atmosphere is similar to that found on a comet. In 2018, scientists from the Southwest Research Institute in Boulder, Colorado, studied data collected from the first flyby of Pluto.

New Horizons photographed the surface of Pluto from a distance of just 7,800 miles (12,500 km).

This illustration combines New Horizons images of Pluto (bottom) and Charon.

The researchers came up with the theory that Pluto may have formed from 1 billion comets all colliding together like a bunch of dirty snowballs.

What's in a Name?

Pluto is orbited by five known moons. The largest, Charon, is about half the size of Pluto itself. Some experts regard Pluto and Charon as a binary, or double, dwarf planet. Charon is loaded with giant canyons and craters similar to those seen on most moons. In 2018, some of Charon's features were named by the International Astronomical Union (IAU). Many of these names honor the spirit of human exploration, pioneering journeys, and mysterious destinations. Some are fictional. Some are real. Argo Chasma is named for the ship sailed by Jason and the Argonauts in Greek mythology. Clarke Montes honors Sir Arthur C. Clarke, a writer who wrote the book *2001: A Space Odyssey*.

CHAPTER 4

Space Telescopes

The Hubble **Space Telescope** (HST) launched in 1990. Since then, it has provided great insight into our universe. It has taken images of objects as close as the Moon and as far as the most **remote**, or faraway, galaxies.

The HST cost $1.5 billion to build, but it almost failed before the first observation was made. It had a flaw in its mirror that had to be repaired in space in 1993. But Hubble went on to become one of the most famous space telescopes ever. After its last servicing in 2009, the HST was expected to keep working until 2015. It outlasted that target and is expected to continue searching space well past 2020.

In the Eye of Hubble

In 1995, astronomers pointed the HST toward an area of space that experts believed was empty. In reality, it turned out to be far from empty! The HST took a picture that contained more than 3,000 galaxies. They were simply too far away to be discovered by any other telescope.

This view from the HST shows a ***nebula****, or a cloud of dust and gas, known as a supernova remnant. They are the remains left over from the explosion of a star.*

An astronaut carries out maintenance on the HST.

The image was named the Hubble Deep Field. Although the HST is used by many astronomers to photograph objects light-years away from Earth, it also takes pictures of other planets in our Solar System. In 2018, the HST focused on Neptune, the farthest known planet. Neptune is 3 billion miles (4.8 billion km) from Earth. Hubble discovered that a massive storm on Neptune is shrinking. The storm was once big enough to cover the whole Atlantic Ocean. Now, scientists believe that if it keeps getting smaller, it will soon be gone. The disappearing weather system is not behaving as scientists had predicted. They thought it would break up with a burst of activity. Instead, it is fading slowly away. The HST is our best connection to distant Neptune at the moment. It is therefore vital for providing the information scientists need to understand the changing weather systems on Neptune.

YOUR MISSION

The storm on Neptune was once big enough to cover the whole Atlantic Ocean. Imagine if a storm that big occurred on Earth. How might it change the way people in the storm's path live? Can you think of any types of storms on Earth that have affected how people live?

Kepler Space Telescope

The Kepler space telescope was launched in 2009. Unlike the HST, Kepler orbited the Sun rather than Earth. Its mission was to observe one area of the universe continuously for a period of four years. The goal was to identify the presence of any planets in that part of the sky that may be similar to Earth. Kepler looked at 100,000 stars similar to our Sun. Kepler's **field of view**, or the part of the sky at which it looked at any one time, was about 30,000 times larger than the HST's field of view. The astronomers using Kepler were waiting for a blink. If one or more of these thousands of stars blink, it might be a sign that a planet is passing in front of them.

Successful Stargazing!

In 2018, researchers using the Kepler space telescope announced that our Solar System now had a challenger for the number of planets orbiting a single star. Kepler had found an eighth planet circling a star named Kepler-90. Kepler-90 is a Sunlike star 2,545 light-years from Earth. The apparent patterns stars make in the sky are called **constellations**. Kepler-90 is in a constellation named Draco, the Dragon.

The Kepler mission took off from Florida on March 7, 2009, onboard a Delta II rocket.

The new planet, Kepler-90i, orbits its star once every 14.4 days. Google used a form of **artificial intelligence (AI)** called machine learning to help sift through the huge amount of data gathered by Kepler. Computers learned to identify planets by noting where the telescope had already identified changes in starlight. The computers used this knowledge to analyze Kepler's data. In four years, Kepler recorded 35,000 blinks of a possible planet passing in front of a star.

Switching It Up

Since its discovery, scientists have confirmed that Kepler-90i is hot. The planet is so close to its star that its average surface temperature is thought to be above 800 °Fahrenheit (427 °C). The planet is about one-third larger than Earth. The remarkable find has encouraged more research. Kepler moved on to an extended mission. Instead of focusing on one piece of space for years, it began switching its field of view about every three months. Kepler is now retired, but new technology, such as AI, is offering more opportunities to understand solar systems beyond our own.

This illustration shows a cloudy exoplanet, a planet outside our Solar System.

A New Telescopic Star

The HST may one day be knocked off its pedestal as the most famous space telescope—if the astronomers and other scientists behind the James Webb Space Telescope (JWST) have their way. The JWST will take over where the earlier telescope left off. Its 21-foot (6.5 m) diameter **primary mirror** will give it a light-collecting area around six-and-a-half times greater than the HST. Its field of view will be about 15 times larger.

Of just as much importance is where it will eventually be located. The HST is in orbit 355 miles (570 km) above Earth. The JWST will not orbit Earth. Instead, it will sit in space more than 930,000 miles (1.5 million km) away. This will enable it to see deeper into space—and therefore further back in time. The farther away an object is, the further back in time we are seeing. The HST can see young galaxies, but the JWST will be able to see galaxies that are only babies.

Scientists examine the primary mirror of the JWST. The mirror is made up of interlocking hexagonal, or six-sided, segments.

Mission Possible

During its first year, the JWST will study Mars. The telescope will investigate how the Red Planet went from once being wet to being dry and dusty today. Orbiters and rovers have already found evidence that liquid water was once found on the planet. Most of that water is now lost. The JWST will try to uncover how much water has been lost.

The JWST is being built in a clean laboratory to avoid any problems with dust. Once it is launched, it will be difficult to make repairs.

MISSION:

Space Science

JWST cost more than $8.8 billion dollars to build—and it overran its scheduled launch by six years. The technology of the JWST is so advanced that NASA delayed the mission to do more testing on the telescope's complex systems. There were also setbacks such as tears in the tennis-court-sized sun shield. These problems have to be solved before launch. The JWST will not be in Earth orbit, so it cannot be serviced by astronauts. It needs to function flawlessly from the moment it reaches its spot in space.

The JWST will investigate how the water cycle works on Mars. This will help scientists understand whether the planet was capable of supporting life in the past, and whether it can support life today. It will also explore methane gas on Mars. These mysterious plumes continue to hint at the possibility of life. The methane could come from bacteria. Data from the JWST will provide new clues to the origin of this gas.

CHAPTER 5

New Discoveries

Scientists now agree that the Moon holds water. A Japanese team has discovered a mineral called moganite from the Moon. They found it in a lunar **meteorite**, which is a Moon rock that lands on Earth. Moganite needs water to form, so the discovery reinforces the idea that water exists on the Moon.

The scientists analyzed 13 different meteorites from the desert areas in Africa to determine the chemical make-up and structure. Only one sample contained moganite. If the mineral had formed in the desert, it would have been in all of the samples. This is the first time that moganite has been found in lunar rocks.

The Quest

Water is vital if humans are to build a self-sustaining settlement on the Moon. JAXA is planning two missions to search for water. In the early 2020s, the first mission would land on one of the Moon's poles, which is a likely source of water or ice. A second mission later in the decade would collect sample rocks from the far side of the Moon, which is the side facing away from Earth.

This photograph from the ISS shows a moonrise, as the Moon rises above the clouds of Earth.

The term moonscape comes from the Moon's airless, dry, dusty landscape.

Life on the Moon?

Today, our Moon is **uninhabitable**, meaning nothing can live there, but what about in the past? An **astrobiologist** from Washington University suggests there may have been two periods in the past when life could have existed on the Moon. Conditions were right for life about 4 billion years ago and again about 3.5 billion years ago. During those times, scientists think the Moon was releasing superhot gases and steam from its interior. Water could have pooled on the surface, and life could have begun on the Moon in much the same way as it did on Earth. Life could also have been carried to the Moon by a meteorite.

MISSION:

Space Science

Scientists at NASA planned a mission to search for water and other useful materials on the Moon. The plan was to send a rover to study samples of soil and rock at the lunar poles. After four years of development, however, NASA canceled the mission in April 2018. It said it wanted instead to develop landers that could carry out multiple missions. This would allow it to locate, dig up, and process minerals across bigger areas of the lunar surface.

Dwarf Planets

Pluto is the best-known dwarf planet. It is too small to be a regular planet but too large to be classified with smaller bodies, such as asteroids.

As of 2018, the IAU recognized five named dwarf planets: Ceres, Pluto, Eris, Haumea, and Makemake. The last four are called **plutoids**. A plutoid is a dwarf planet that orbits farther from the Sun than Neptune. Plutoids are also sometimes called ice dwarfs because they are all small and cold. Ceres is unique. At only 590 miles (950 km) in diameter, it is the only dwarf planet in the inner Solar System.

And There's More!

There probably are many other dwarf planets in our Solar System. Sedna, Quaoar, and 2012 VP113 are three examples of bodies that may one day be recognized as dwarf planets. 2012 VP113 is thought to have one of the most distant orbits found beyond the known edge of our Solar System.

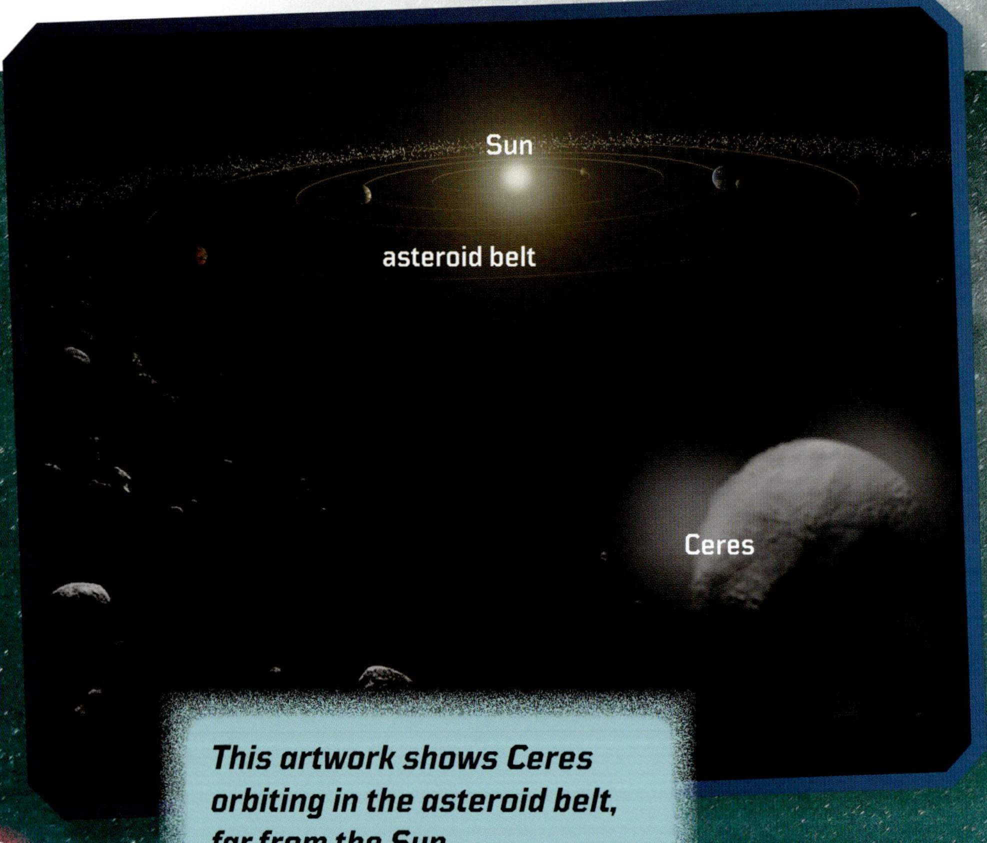

This artwork shows Ceres orbiting in the asteroid belt, far from the Sun.

This mosaic includes some of the features Dawn discovered on Ceres.

NASA scientists think there could be more than 100 dwarf planets waiting to be discovered. One is nicknamed DeeDee, which is formally known as object 2014 UZ224. Observations in 2017 suggest that it might be a candidate for dwarf-planet status.

Carbon on Ceres

In 2017, scientists behind NASA's Dawn mission announced that they had found **organic material** on Ceres. Organic material is based on atoms of **carbon**, which is an element found in all living things. The discovery does not mean there was—or is—life on Ceres, but it is interesting. How did this material get onto the surface of Ceres? In addition, how is organic material distributed across our Solar System?

The material on Ceres was found using a visible and infrared **spectrometer**, a device that analyzes sunlight. The instrument detects which colors of sunlight are reflected and which are absorbed. This gives clues about what type of material is on Ceres. To begin with, it seemed there was only a small amount of organic material on the dwarf planet, but that figure has now been increased.

The Kuiper Belt

The Kuiper Belt is like a **cosmic** doughnut that surrounds our Solar System beyond the orbit of Neptune. It is full of what are called Kuiper Belt objects. Scientists estimate that the Kuiper Belt contains as many as 200 dwarf planets, a trillion or more comets, and hundreds of thousands of other small bodies made largely of ice. Several of the dwarf planets found in the Kuiper Belt have moons.

NASA's New Horizons became the first probe to explore the Kuiper Belt when it flew beyond Pluto in 2015. At the start of 2019, the probe was scheduled to fly past another Kuiper Belt object, called 2014 MU69 but nicknamed Ultima Thule. It would be the most distant object in our Solar System to be visited by a spacecraft.

Several Kuiper Belt objects have strange orbits. Astronomers believe this might reflect the gravitational pull of a large object that has not yet been discovered. They believe this object might not be a dwarf planet, comet, or asteroid, but a full-sized ninth planet.

The Hunt for Planet Nine

Astronomers have been searching for a Planet Nine for the past few years. The evidence that something at the edge of our Solar System has a big gravitational pull might be a clue. Researchers at Caltech believe they have found mathematical evidence of a ninth planet deep in our Solar System. If this planet exists, it would have a mass 10 times that of Earth and may take between 10,000 and 20,000 years to make one full orbit around the Sun.

This artwork shows New Horizons (top right) passing 2014 MU69. This Kuiper Belt object orbits 1 billion miles (1.6 billion km) beyond Pluto.

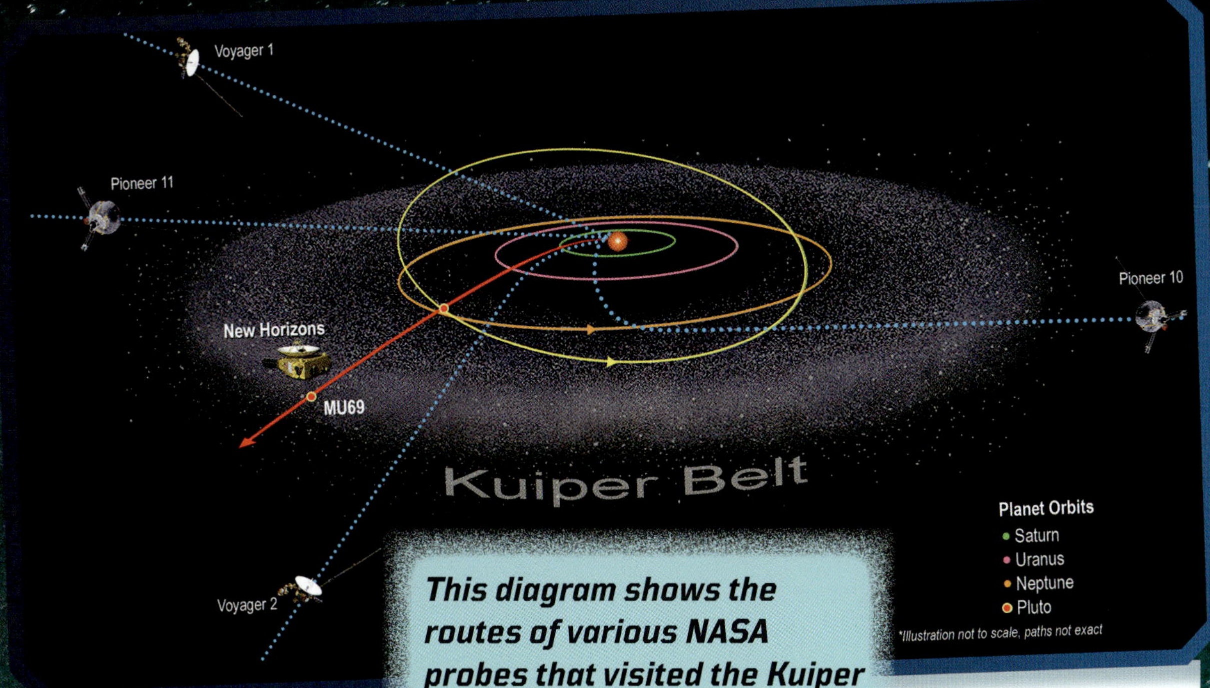

This diagram shows the routes of various NASA probes that visited the Kuiper Belt beyond the planets.

Other researchers have their doubts. The Caltech evidence is based on mathematical models and computer **simulations**, or patterns, rather than direct astronomical observations. Some researchers believe the strange orbits of Kuiper Belt objects are not caused by the gravity of a mysterious ninth planet at all. They think the movements are due to objects bumping into each other, like bumper cars at a carnival, throwing them out of their normal orbits. Astronomers are using the world's most powerful telescopes to search for Planet Nine. If it exists, they will find it. If not, they will start searching for other reasons for the mysterious pull at the edge of our Solar System.

YOUR MISSION

You have read about the different opinions surrounding the existence of Planet Nine. Do you think it exists? Why or why not? Explain your reasoning.

CHAPTER 6

What's Next?

NASA has been studying Saturn and its moons for more than 10 years. One of the most interesting subjects they have investigated is Saturn's largest moon, Titan. Titan is of particular interest to researchers because it holds liquid. There are oceans, rivers, and lakes made of liquid methane and ethane. But the real secret of Titan lies underground—and exploring it will mean going deep.

In 2004, NASA's Cassini mission showed that Titan is hiding an ocean of liquid water and **ammonia** beneath its surface. ESA's Huygens lander also found evidence to suggest that a watery ocean exists 23 to 50 miles (55–80 km) below Titan's surface. This would mean that Titan might possibly have environments capable of supporting life.

NASA has plans to explore Titan's surface seas by first sending a submarine there within the next 20 years. To be successful, a submarine would have to be able to withstand temperatures as low as -300 °Fahrenheit (-184 °C). It would also need to be able to function in an ocean made of liquid methane and ethane. The submarine will have to be self-operating, as it will be beyond human control. It will need to study ocean conditions, move around sea beds, and operate below the surface. Building such a submarine will be an engineering feat.

Scientists noticed clouds forming in the atmosphere of Titan. It might be a clue to the materials on Titan's surface.

This image of Titan's rocky mountains was captured by the lander Huygens as it neared the moon's surface.

Building Models

Washington State University researchers are currently working with NASA to figure how this technology might work in Titan's extreme environment. The team built a tank to hold an "ocean" of liquid methane and ethane at temperatures similar to those on Titan. They added a tiny heated cylinder to test what might happen to a submarine in Titan's oceans. The researchers even figured out how to record video in these challenging conditions. It took a lot of creativity, but their work is not yet done. They are continuing to work with NASA to make the submarine a reality in the near future.

MISSION:

Space Science

Cassini discovered a few of Titan's secrets, but it also discovered something else—another moon orbiting Saturn. The planet has a total of 62 moons, ranging from the giant Titan to tiny moonlets that are only 1,300 feet (400 m) wide. Cassini's images showed a small, previously unknown moon growing from bits of icy material on its surface.

Is Anyone Out There?

Does life exist outside of Earth? The search for **extraterrestrial** life has been the subject of many science fiction movies and books. In reality, "life" does not necessarily mean humanlike. In most cases, scientists are searching for microscopic bacteria. Researchers at the University of California and the University of Southern Queensland in Australia are researching faraway moons. They have found more than 100 giant planets in other solar systems that have the potential to have moons that could support life. Their work is important for guiding the design of future telescopes.

Looking to the Clouds

A team of researchers at the University of Wisconsin-Madison's Space Science and Engineering Center is looking up to the clouds of Venus in the hunt for extraterrestrial life. The idea that the clouds might be home to life was first suggested in 1967 by the scientists Harold Morowitz and Carl Sagan. In 2018, researchers revisited the theory with data to support it. Microbes can be found almost everywhere on Earth, from hot springs to the cold depths of the ocean. They have also been encountered in toxic mud in ponds near mines.

This image shows the swirling clouds above Venus. Could the cloudy planet be home to life?

Venus is covered in thick clouds. Some experts believe they might be home to life forms that bloom and fade like algae, simple plants that grow in water on Earth.

Tiny bacteria have even been located as high as 25 miles (40 km) into our atmosphere. While scientists already know the surface conditions of Venus will not support life, the planet's clouds are another story. These clouds have dark streaks or patches that are known to absorb light. What is making them do that? The particles that make up the patches in the clouds are the same size as some bacteria on Earth. Scientists wonder whether bacteria might be absorbing the light on Venus.

Collecting Necessary Data

NASA may learn more from Russia's Venera-D mission in the late 2020s. The Venus Atmospheric Maneuverable Platform (VAMP) is a spaceship being developed by Northrop Grumman Corporation in the United States. VAMP flies like a plane but can also float like a blimp. It could hang out in the clouds for long periods of time. This would be the perfect vehicle for sampling the clouds. If it is built, the next step would be to get it up into space.

ACTIVITY

Your Space Science Mission

Our Solar System is vast. It is so large that our current technology is incapable of carrying humans far beyond our planetary neighbor, Mars. In the future, however, space scientists hope that they will develop new types of spacecraft and engines that will make it possible to explore the distant regions of our Solar System. If that came to pass, where would you choose to go?

Imagine that humans could travel anywhere within our Solar System. Research how many hours, days, or years it would take for humans to reach each of the planets, or Pluto and the dwarf planets in the Kuiper Belt. In this book, you have read about the different types of objects that all orbit our Sun. Now it is your turn to design a mission to explore deep into our Solar System!

Planning Your Mission

1 Choose your destination.
Using reliable Internet sources such as NASA, make a list of the known planets, dwarf planets, moons, asteroids, and comets within our Solar System. Which would you choose to visit? Would it be one of the hot, rocky planets near the Sun, an outer planet, or a dwarf planet orbiting in the cold darkness beyond Neptune?

2 Set your goals.
What are you going to investigate? Are you going to look for signs of life in the clouds of Venus, or dig for valuable minerals on the moons of Jupiter?

3 Choose your instruments.
Depending on your goals, think about what devices you might need to carry on your mission. Would you need drills and tools to analyze rocks from the surface? Or heat shields to protect you from the Sun? Would you need a rover to explore the surface of a planet or a moon?

4 Plan your trip.
Research the fastest spacecraft available. Figure out how long it would take to reach your chosen destination using current engine technology. If you set out today, would you even live long enough to reach your destination? If not, how would humans be able to carry out such long journeys into space? Could astronauts bring up children onboard their spacecraft to carry on their mission? What would be the pros and cons?

5 Collaborate!
Brainstorm ways you could get a human to the far reaches of our Solar System within his or her lifetime. Share your ideas with some friends. See if they can come up with any better ideas about exploring the farthest parts of our Solar System.

Glossary

Please note: Some **bold-faced** words are defined where they appear in the book.

acidic Containing damaging chemicals

ammonia A colorless, strong-smelling gas

artificial intelligence (AI) The use of computers to "think" like humans

asteroids Rocky bodies that orbit the Sun

astrobiologist Someone who studies life in space

astronomers People who study space and the universe

atoms The smallest particles of a substance that can exist

bacteria Tiny organisms that may cause disease

comets Bodies made of ice and dust that travel around the Sun

contaminating Making something impure

corrode To eat away with chemicals

cosmic Related to the universe

dwarf planets Small bodies that orbit a star

element A chemical that cannot be broken down

equator An imaginary line around a sphere

extraterrestrial Existing beyond Earth

flybys Voyages past bodies in space

gravity A force that attracts all objects toward one another

infrared A type of radiation that is invisible to the human eye

interstellar Existing in space between stars

landers Spacecraft designed to land on bodies in space

magnetic field A region with a magnetic charge

mass The amount of matter in an object

meteorite A rock from space that lands on Earth or another body in space

microbes Tiny organisms

moons Space bodies that orbit planets

orbit A path taken by one body around another

outer planets The planets farthest from the Sun

planets Bodies in space that orbit stars

poles The "top" and "bottom" extremes of a spherical body such as a planet

primary mirror The part of a telescope that gathers light from space

radar A method for locating objects using radio waves

reactors Plants for generating energy

resources Useful materials

robotic Able to perform mechanical tasks based on programmed instructions

satellites Natural or artificial objects that orbit a planet or star

solar furnace A structure that uses mirrors to focus sunlight and produce heat

solar panels Panels that turn sunlight into energy

space telescope A telescope based in space

telescopes Instruments that gather information about distant objects

water cycle The process by which water moves from the oceans to the sky and falls as rain

Learning More

Books

Bow, James. *Space Entrepreneurs* (Science and Technology Start-Up Stars). Crabtree Publishing Company, 2018.

Dakers, Diane. *Chris Hadfield: Inspiring New Generations to Explore Space* (Crabtree Groundbreaker Biographies). Crabtree Publishing Company, 2015.

Gifford, Clive. *Astronomy, Astronauts, and Space Exploration* (Watch This Space!). Crabtree Publishing Company, 2015.

Gifford, Clive. *The Solar System, Meteors, and Comets* (Watch This Space!). Crabtree Publishing Company, 2015.

Space! (Knowledge Encyclopedia) DK Children, 2015.

Websites

Find out about the work of space telescopes and what they are teaching us about our Solar System:

amazingspace.org

Any questions about our Solar System? Find answers from professional astronomers here:

coolcosmos.ipac.caltech.edu/asks

Want to discover what NASA has planned for exploring our Solar System and beyond? Look here:

https://spaceplace.nasa.gov/menu/solar-system

Go here to find a list of missions to explore our Solar System, both past and present:

www.planetary.org/explore/space-topics/space-missions/

Index

About the Author

Megan Kopp is a children's book writer who lives in the Rocky Mountains. While she enjoys reading and writing about space science, she has her feet firmly planted on the ground!